Clarity Publishers
Birmingham, AL

Life Bible Study
P. O. Box 36040
Birmingham, AL 35236

To order additional copies of this resource, call the publisher at 877.265.1605 or order online at www.lifebiblestudy.com.

Roberta Watson

Roberta Watson is a graduate of New Orleans Baptist Theological Seminary (NOBTS) and has served as an adjunct professor at the NOBTS North Georgia extension center. With nearly 20 years of ministry experience, she has served in a variety of educational ministries in churches in Texas and Georgia. She has also partnered with State and local Baptist Associations to provide leadership support and training to the local church.

Roberta has worked as a free-lance writer for many years providing curriculum materials for several national organizations. She has also worked as an editor of Bible curriculum and has written extensively for Clarity Publishers.

She and her husband, Todd, have been married for more than 20 years. Their daughter, Katie, is a college student, and their son, Will, is a high school student. They enjoy supporting their kids' school, extracurricular, and church activities. Her favorite vacation experience was watching the sunrise over the Sea of Galilee.

Editoral & Design Staff

Editor
Margie Williamson

Copy Editor
Jason Odom

Art Director
Brandi Etheredge

Graphic Designer
Laurel-Dawn B. McBurney

TABLE of CONTENTS

how to use this book

This study has been designed to help you prepare for a group Bible Study experience, to use during a group Bible Study experience, or as an individual Bible study guide. Every lesson is divided into five sections; each section concludes with a devotional suggestion and journaling activity. To get the most from this study, consider the following suggestions:

1. Gather your favorite Bible, a pen or pencil, and a highlighter before you begin. As you study the lesson, stop and read the assigned passage first. You will have the opportunity to dig deeper into some verses at the end of each section.

2. Use the learner commentary and sidebars to guide your personal Bible study.

3. Complete each day's study with the devotional suggestions and journaling assignments at the end of each section. Allow God this time to transform you through your study and your time with Him.

4. Take your book along to your small group study. The discussion suggestions will be helpful to you during your study time.

Be prepared to consider, examine, and evaluate God's Word as you move through this study. Our prayer is that this study will give you the opportunity to better understand what God had in mind when He designed us to be human.

intro

On the eve of His crucifixion, Jesus tried to prepare His disciples for the events of the next three days. After explaining that He was returning to His Father, Jesus promised that He would send another Counselor to be with His followers forever. Through the presence of the Holy Spirit, Jesus' followers would never be alone (see John 14). On the day of Pentecost, Jesus' promise was fulfilled—the Spirit descended upon the believers and began His ministry among God's people on earth (see Acts 2). Later, the apostle Paul explained that the presence of the Holy Spirit was God's seal on His people—a deposit that guaranteed their inheritance as joint heirs with Christ (see Eph. 1).

The apostles experienced the presence and power of the Holy Spirit as they labored for the kingdom of God. Through their writings, they encouraged all Christians to fully surrender to the Holy Spirit, who equips them to fulfill their ministry calling and strengthens them to live their faith in a world filled with sin. In this study, six distinct roles of the Spirit will be examined:

• Believers are called to be holy because God is holy. Through the presence of the Spirit of holiness, the sinful desires of humanity are replaced by the Spirit's desire for holiness.

• Believers are told to love others, even their enemies and people who persecute them. By the power of the Spirit of love, believers are filled with God's love for all people and compelled to share God's love by telling others of their faith.

• Believers are promised that they will know the truth and the truth will set them free. Through the instruction of the Spirit of truth, believers can understand and apply the truths of Scripture to their lives so they can live free from Satan's influences.

• Believers are told they must be born again to be saved. Through the work of the Spirit of life, believers are granted new spiritual life at the moment of salvation. As believers walk in the Spirit of life, the power of sin is defeated. Upon their physical death, the Spirit of life grants eternal life to all believers.

• Believers are challenged to walk in wisdom each day. Through the ministry of the Spirit of wisdom and revelation, believers continue to gain understanding of the character of God and the wisdom that He provides. The Spirit reveals the deep things of God—in the form of spiritual truths—to all believers so they can apply God's wisdom to their lives.

• Believers are called to bring glory to God in everything they do. Through the presence of the Spirit of glory, believers learn to conduct their lives to insure God's glory is revealed. When believers face persecution for their faith, the Spirit of glory gives them strength and peace to endure.

Jesus' promise has been fulfilled. Believers are SEALED with the Holy Spirit as a mark of their salvation and a promise for eternal life. Believers are not abandoned as orphans because the Holy Spirit dwells within believers to guide their actions, equip them for ministry, and strengthen their faith. Through the presence of the Holy Spirit, believers become powerful citizens of the kingdom of God on earth as they wait to see the fullness of God's glory in heaven.

8 essential truths

GOD IS
Only one true and living God exists. He is the Creator of the universe, eternally existing in three Persons—the Father, Son, and Holy Spirit—each equally deserving of humanity's worship and obedience. He is infinite and perfect in all His attributes.

THE BIBLE IS GOD'S WORD
The Bible is God's written revelation to people, divinely given through human authors who were inspired by the Holy Spirit. It is entirely true. The Bible is totally sufficient and completely authoritative for matters of life and faith. The goal of God's Word is the restoration of humanity into His image.

PEOPLE ARE GOD'S TREASURE
God created people in His image for His glory. They are the crowning work of His creation. Yet every person has willfully disobeyed God—an act known as sin—thus inheriting both physical and spiritual death and the need for salvation. All human beings are born with a sin-nature and into an environment inclined toward sin. Only by the grace of God through Jesus Christ can they experience salvation.

JESUS IS GOD AND SAVIOR
Jesus is both fully God and fully human. He is Christ, the Son of God. Born of a virgin, He lived a sinless life and performed many miracles. He died on the cross to provide people forgiveness of sin and eternal salvation. Jesus rose from the dead, ascended to the right hand of the Father, and will return in power and glory.

THE HOLY SPIRIT IS GOD & EMPOWERER
The Holy Spirit is supernatural and sovereign, baptizing all believers into the Body of Christ. He lives within all Christians beginning at the moment of salvation and then empowers them for bold witness and effective service as they yield to Him. The Holy Spirit convicts individuals of sin, uses God's Word to mature believers into Christ-likeness, and secures them until Christ returns.

SALVATION IS BY FAITH ALONE
All human beings are born with a sin nature, separated from God, and in need of a Savior. That salvation comes only through a faith relationship with Jesus Christ, the Savior, as a person repents of sin and receives Christ's forgiveness and eternal life. Salvation is instantaneous and accomplished solely by the power of the Holy Spirit through the Word of God. This salvation is wholly of God by grace on the basis of the shed blood of Jesus Christ and not on the basis of human works. All the redeemed are secure in Christ forever.

THE CHURCH IS GOD'S PLAN
The Holy Spirit immediately places all people who put their faith in Jesus Christ into one united spiritual body, the Church, of which Christ is the head. The primary expression of the Church on earth is in autonomous local congregations of baptized believers. The purpose of the Church is to glorify God by taking the gospel to the entire world and by building its members up in Christ-likeness through the instruction of God's Word, fellowship, service, worship, and prayer.

THE FUTURE IS IN GOD'S HANDS
God is actively involved in our lives and our future. Through His prophets, God announced His plans for the future redemption of His people through the life, death, and resurrection of His Son. With the call of the disciples, God prepared the way for the future of His Church. In Scripture, God promised that Jesus Christ will return personally and visibly in glory to the earth to resurrect and judge the saved and unsaved. As the all-knowing and all-powerful Creator and Judge, God can and should be trusted today, and with our future.

week 1

the spirit of holiness

BIBLICAL PASSAGE: Romans 1:1-6

SUPPORTING PASSAGES: Acts 3:24-26; Romans 8:11; Galatians 1:11-12; 1 Peter 3:18

MEMORY VERSE: 1 Peter 1:15-16

BIBLICAL TRUTH: As part of the Trinity, the Holy Spirit imparts holiness through His presence and power in the lives of believers.

CONSIDER

Every week, Christians around the world assemble to worship God, to pray for His guidance, and to hear a message from the Scriptures to prepare them for another week of life. Many Christians understand the depth of God's love for them, which is revealed through Jesus' sacrifice to provide their salvation. But many believers do not fully comprehend the power of the Holy Spirit, much less rely upon Him to guide them through the challenges of each day. As a result, no matter their good intentions, within hours of worship, many have already said or done something that would not be pleasing to God. Instead of living the abundant life that Jesus promised, they are living in hopelessness and defeat.

Jesus understands the challenges believers face as they try to live holy lives that please God. For this reason, Jesus personally relied upon the presence and power of the Spirit of holiness as He walked this planet. As a result, He lived a sinless life that fully pleased His Father. As you study this passage of Scripture, consider these things: Is your walk with God where you want it to be? In what areas are you struggling to become or remain obedient to Him? How could the power of the Spirit of holiness change your life?

Choosing to Serve Christ

The apostle Paul recognized the significant life-change that happens when a person places their faith in Jesus Christ. Prior to his conversion, Paul was known as Saul and was feared as the Pharisee who persecuted Christians. But when he met the risen Christ and accepted Him as Lord of his life, Paul became a new person. He surrendered his life completely to Christ and considered himself a servant fully devoted to fulfilling his Master's plan for his life.

In his letter to the Romans, Paul set forth the gospel in the clearest of terms. Those who are called to follow Jesus as Lord will serve Him unselfishly, obey Him without questions, and spread the gospel to others. In return, the same Holy Spirit that empowered Jesus for His earthly ministry will equip and enable His followers for their ministry.

sealed

THE CALL TO HOLINESS

Read 1 Peter 1:13-16. Peter emphasized God's call for His followers to be holy because He is holy. For Peter, this call involved preparing our minds for action, exercising self-control, and remaining obedient – all by remaining focused on the grace received from Jesus Christ. As you journal below, consider: What do you think is necessary for living a holy life? How can you prepare your mind for obedience? In what areas of life do you need to exercise greater self-control?

We are called to *serve* God by spreading the gospel of Jesus Christ.

Spreading the Gospel

Romans 1:1-13

Because Paul never had the opportunity to visit or teach in the community of believers at Rome, he wrote this letter to them. In the opening verses of his letter, Paul established his credentials as both a servant and an apostle of Jesus Christ. As a servant (also translated bond-servant or slave), Paul had chosen to set aside his own will for a lifetime of service to his Master, Jesus Christ. As an apostle, a term given to those who were appointed by Jesus as His witnesses to the world, Paul was authorized to preach, to teach, and to establish and discipline churches. This dual identity emphasized Paul's great humility and great authority, and enabled him to fulfill both the responsibilities and privileges of spreading the gospel.

Having introduced himself, Paul immediately began to explain God's plan for bringing salvation to humanity through His Son, Jesus Christ. By emphasizing that the gospel fulfilled God's promises revealed "through his prophets in the Holy Scriptures," Paul refuted any suspicions that he created the gospel message or that Israel's refusal to accept Jesus as the Messiah destroyed God's original plan. Throughout the course of his letter, Paul extensively related the Old Testament promises to God's plan for salvation.

APOSTLE (APOSTOLOS)
was a term used by Jesus to designate the men He personally chose to serve as His ambassadors or witnesses as they carried the gospel to the nations. The apostles were given authority to preach and teach, as well as to establish, supervise, and discipline churches.

SERVANT (DOULOS)
was a term used to identify a servant, a bondservant, or a slave. The servant or slave assumes a lifelong position of service to another. The will of the servant is completely set aside so that he might fulfill the will of the master.

react

How would you define your relationship with Jesus Christ? What are some of the responsibilities and privileges that believers must fulfill as they share the gospel today?

WITNESSING IN POWER

Read Acts 1:8; Ephesians 6:18-20; and Colossians 4:3-4. Jesus told His disciples to wait for the Spirit to empower them as His witnesses. Paul understood that he needed to rely upon the Spirit when he shared the gospel. He frequently asked others to pray for him to share the gospel with boldness and power. As you journal below, consider: What role does prayer and the Holy Spirit play in your witnessing efforts? What might happen if you joined with other believers to pray for boldness and power from the Spirit before you shared the gospel?

PAUSE to PRAY

Share with God your fears about sharing the gospel. Pray for the Holy Spirit to prepare others to hear the gospel. Praise God for the times when the Spirit helped you lead someone to Christ.

Empowered *by the* Spirit

Romans 1:3-4

For those familiar with the prophecies concerning the Messiah, Paul explained that Jesus, in His human form, was a descendant from the line of David (see Is. 7:14; 9:6-7; and 11:1-3). Matthew traced Jesus' ancestral lineage from His earthly father, Joseph, back to David (see Matt. 1:1-16). Luke traced Jesus' lineage through His mother, Mary, back to David (see Luke 3:23-31). Jesus was also the Son of God, proven when the Spirit of holiness raised Him from the dead. In these two verses, Paul revealed Jesus' dual nature—fully human, yet also, fully divine.

Jesus lived on earth in a body of flesh, and yet was fully surrendered to the presence and power of the Spirit of holiness. R. A. Torrey suggested that the term "Holy Spirit" refers to the inherent moral character of God the Spirit, while the term "Spirit of holiness" reveals that the Spirit is willing and able to convey holiness to others. Through the power of the Spirit of holiness, Jesus was guided and sustained during His earthly ministry, which allowed Him to remain fully obedient through numerous trials and tests before His final act of obedience— death on the cross. Because The Holy Spirit is God and Empowerer, Jesus relied upon the Spirit's power as He lived a sinless life, offered Himself as the atoning sacrifice for sin, and was resurrected from the dead and seated at His Father's right hand (see Heb. 1:3; 9:11-15). For this reason, Jesus Christ is Lord.

"This unique person, seed of David and Son of God, weak and powerful, incarnate and exalted, is Jesus (a human, historical figure), Christ (the Messiah of the Old Testament Scripture), our Lord, who owns and rules our lives." John R. W. Stott

interactive

Read the Scriptures identified below and list ways the Holy Spirit empowered Jesus' life and ministry:

Luke 1:30-35 _____

Luke 3:21-22 _____

Luke 4:14-19 _____

Isaiah 11:2-3 _____

Hebrews 9:14 _____

Romans 8:11 _____

Acts 1:2-8 _____

4

(Answers are provided on page 8.)

react

How would you define your relationship with Jesus Christ? What are some of the responsibilities and privileges that believers must fulfill as they share the gospel today?

SURRENDER TO THE SPIRIT

Read Romans 8:9-11. People who have received salvation by placing their faith in Jesus Christ have also received the gift of the indwelling Holy Spirit. The Spirit who resurrected Jesus from the dead is the same Spirit that empowers us to live righteously before God. As you journal below, consider: In what areas of life are you still struggling between the desires of the flesh and the desires of the Spirit? What do you need to do to surrender those struggles to the control of the Spirit of holiness?

PAUSE to PRAY

Confess your struggles to live righteously before God. Pray for the willingness to surrender control of those areas of your life to the Holy Spirit. Thank God that you no longer have to fight those battles in your own strength.

We are empowered by the Holy Spirit to walk in *obedience* to God.

Walking *in* Obedience

Romans 1:5-6

Paul reiterated his assertion that through Jesus and for His sake, he received grace as well as the appointment as an apostle to the Gentiles. Paul consistently, through his preaching and his writings, affirmed that salvation and forgiveness of sins through Jesus Christ was available to everyone, people from all nations, who confess Jesus as Lord and believe that God raised Him from the dead (see Rom. 10:9-10). Paul seemed to make one distinction. While he was called as an apostle, his readers were called to belong to Jesus Christ. But Paul didn't allow followers of Christ to be satisfied with receiving salvation. He called them to full obedience to Christ as evidence of their faith in Him.

sealed

Through His magnificent grace, God gives believers the gift of salvation, which is expressed through their faith in Jesus. For believers fully committed to Jesus as Lord of their lives, faith cannot exist without the desire to obey His commands. Paul also revealed that followers of Christ were called to be saints (Rom. 1:7). By definition, a saint is one who is holy, set apart, sanctified, and consecrated to God. Saints are called to share in God's holiness while refusing to participate in the sinful actions of the world. Thankfully, when Jesus returned to heaven, He sent the Spirit to empower His followers to walk in obedience to His commands. When believers allow the Spirit of holiness full control of their lives, they are able to live in ways that please God.

interactive

List some areas in which you currently struggle to obey God.

List some areas where you currently struggle to obey God. How does your flesh, your human desires, lead you to respond to these situations? How would the Spirit lead you to respond in these situations?

respond

Why is obedience to Christ's commands an important part of the believer's lifestyle? How is a Christian's testimony damaged when they teach salvation through Christ but fail to obey His teachings? How can a believer rely upon the Holy Spirit to help them obey Christ's commands?

Read Galatians 5:16-17, 22-25. In these verses, Paul described the continuing battle every Christian faces between the desires of their sinful nature and the desires of the Spirit of holiness within them. He urged believers to surrender to the Spirit who would produce righteous fruit in their lives. As you journal below, consider: How frequently are you aware of the battle between sin and holiness in your life? What are the consequences of choosing your own ways? What fruit has the Spirit produced in your life when you allowed Him complete control?

PAUSE to PRAY

Thank God for the Holy Spirit who dwells within you. Pray for the desire to hear and submit to the Spirit's leading, thereby defeating the sinful desires of the flesh.

Be Holy *because* God *is* Holy

Since God began calling people to follow Him, He has required that they be holy because He is holy. Yet people have consistently proven their inability to be holy. For this reason, God sent His Son to earth in human form. Jesus set aside His deity and walked this planet within the confines of a human body with all its weaknesses. Yet because Jesus walked in perfect unity with the Holy Spirit, He was able to do what had never been done— He lived a sinless life. When He submitted to His Father's will, even to death on a cross, He was found the perfect sacrifice to atone for humanity's sin. As a result, the Spirit of holiness raised Him from the dead and He ascended into heaven. But Jesus had promised that He would never leave or forsake His followers. He sent the Spirit to indwell every believer, so that all might walk in complete obedience to His Father's will.

review

Because Jesus was fully human, He relied upon the presence and power of the Holy Spirit in His life to remain obedient to God in all circumstances. If Jesus relied on the Holy Spirit, how much more should we, His disciples, rely upon the Holy Spirit to live in obedience to God. Why do you think it is so hard for humans to surrender their will to the Holy Spirit? What do you believe are important steps in the process of surrender? What evidence have you seen of the Holy Spirit in your life? Where do you need to surrender more of your will to the Spirit's control?

SURRENDER TO THE SPIRIT

Read Romans 8:9-11. People who have received salvation by placing their faith in Jesus Christ have also received the gift of the indwelling Holy Spirit. The Spirit who resurrected Jesus from the dead is the same Spirit that empowers us to live righteously before God. As you journal below, consider: In what areas of life are you still struggling between the desires of the flesh and the desires of the Spirit? What do you need to do to surrender those struggles to the control of the Spirit of holiness?

PAUSE to PRAY

Confess your struggles to live righteously before God. Pray for the willingness to surrender control of those areas of your life to the Holy Spirit. Thank God that you no longer have to fight those battles in your own strength.

PAGE 4 ANSWERS

Luke 1:30-35 – Mary conceived Jesus by the power of the Holy Spirit.
Luke 3:21-22 – The Holy Spirit descended upon Jesus at His baptism.
Luke 4:14-19 – Jesus was led by the Holy Spirit and empowered to teach, heal, and forgive.
Isaiah 11:2-3 – The Holy Spirit bestowed wisdom, understanding, and power to Jesus.

Hebrews 9:14 – Under the power of the Holy Spirit, Jesus lived a sinless life to offer Himself as an unblemished sacrifice for our sins.
Romans 8:11 – The Holy Spirit raised Jesus from the dead
Acts 1:2-8 – Jesus speaks to His followers through the Holy Spirit, empowering them as His witnesses.

week 2

the spirit of love

BIBLICAL PASSAGE: 2 Timothy 1:3-7

SUPPORTING PASSAGES: Acts 16:1-5; 1 Corinthians 13:1-13; 1 Corinthians 16:10-11; Galatians 5:22-23; 1 John 3:21-24

MEMORY VERSE: 2 Timothy 1:7

BIBLICAL TRUTH: The Holy Spirit enables us to serve God and love people without fear by filling us with the Spirit of love.

CONSIDER

Every day believers are walking and talking witnesses for Christ. Through their actions and their words, they have the opportunity to make their faith in Christ known to others and to invite them to know Christ for themselves. While some believers seem to effortlessly lead people to Christ, others remain tongue-tied. Still others have tried to live and share their faith, but have been ridiculed or rejected so many times that they fear any opportunities to express their faith.

Paul understood the fear that many Christians experience when given the opportunity to express their faith through words or actions. But Paul discovered the antidote to fear and he shared that in this letter to Timothy. Paul realized that his love for God, and the Spirit of love dwelling within him, conquered all fears. Under the control of the Spirit, Paul willingly risked everything, even his life, so that he could tell others of God's amazing love.

A Faithful Mentor

Paul and Timothy had been co-laborers for Christ for approximately twenty years when Paul sent this letter to Timothy. Paul met Timothy during his first missionary journey (c. 46-48 AD). When Paul preached in the town of Lystra, Timothy, his mother, and his grandmother became Christians. When Paul passed through Lystra on his second missionary journey (c. 49-50), he invited Timothy to join him in carrying the gospel to the Gentiles. Paul became Timothy's father in the faith. Timothy traveled with him preaching the gospel and establishing churches throughout Asia Minor. At various times, Paul entrusted Timothy with leading the churches in Thessalonica, Corinth, and Philippi. Paul was in a Roman prison when he wrote this final letter to Timothy encouraging him to serve God faithfully no matter the cost.

THE IMPORTANCE OF MENTORING

Read Titus 2:1-12. Paul placed great emphasis on the importance of older (spiritually mature) men and women teaching younger men and women the basics of faith. By pairing older and younger Christians, Paul emphasized the importance of the mentoring relationship among believers. As you journal below, consider: Who are the people who have mentored you in the faith? How did their instruction help you reach greater levels of spiritual maturity? How can you share what you have learned with others?

PAUSE to PRAY

Thank God that He allows us to learn from people who have walked with Him. Ask God to provide a mentor for you even as He gives you a younger believer to mentor.

Love for God is the foundation for our faith.

The Foundations of Faith

2 Tim. 1:3

Paul stated that he served God just as his forefathers did, showing that the God of the Jewish faith was also the God of the Christian faith. From his forefathers, Paul had been schooled in the Jewish scriptures. He was an Israelite, born in the tribe of Benjamin, who fulfilled the duties of a Pharisee (Phil. 3:5-6). Prior to meeting Jesus on the road to Damascus, Paul persecuted those who followed Christ. When Paul met the resurrected Christ, he recognized Him as the promised Messiah, the one who would save Israel (see Acts 13:16-39). Paul immediately began to preach the gospel of Christ with the same passion and intensity that he had once kept the Law. Paul was not torn between his religious heritage and his knowledge of Christ. Paul's love for God, nurtured through his obedience to the Law and his love for Christ that resulted from his powerful salvation experience, formed the foundation for his ministry. Paul's conscience was clear—cleansed by Jesus—as he boldly preached the gospel throughout Asia Minor.

Paul's love for God spilled over into his loving concern for fellow Christians. Even as Paul served God, he continually prayed for Timothy, his "dear son" in the faith. Sitting in his lonely Roman jail cell, persecuted for his faith in Christ, Paul didn't focus on his own needs but prayed for the needs of others. His prayers were powerful and effective because he knew Timothy's strengths and weaknesses, the ministry challenges that Timothy faced in Ephesus, and the persecution that all Christians faced at that time.

10

react

How is it possible to serve God with a clear, or pure, conscience? Besides prayer, what other ways does your love for God impact your love for people? What happens when Christians pray continually and specifically for other believers?

A GATHERING OF BELIEVERS

Read Hebrews 10:22-25. Because Jesus secured forgiveness for our sins, we can approach God with a sincere heart. Because we are one in heart with other believers, when we gather as His people, we can encourage and strengthen each other toward love and good deeds. As you journal below, consider: Do you faithfully gather with other believers for prayer, worship, and study? What can you do to encourage someone else? How can you draw strength from other believers?

PAUSE to PRAY

Thank God for the believers in your church, community, and family. Pray that God will use you to strengthen and encourage someone else.

sealed

Love for other believers provides a ***community*** where faith is strengthened.

A Community of Faith

2 Tim. 1:4-5

When Paul and Timothy had last parted, Timothy was unable to hold back his tears. Now Paul longed, a feeling similar to homesickness, to see Timothy again. Paul said that he would be filled with joy when he was reunited with Timothy. In fact, three times in this letter, he urged Timothy to come to him (1:4; 4:9; 4:21). When believers are suffering or feeling downtrodden, gathering with other beloved Christians provides the blessings of encouragement and renewed strength.

Timothy's spiritual heritage was similar to Paul's heritage. Though Timothy's father was a Greek (Acts 16:1), his Jewish mother and grandmother had raised Timothy according to the sacred writings of the Old Testament. Like Paul, Timothy was prepared to hear and respond to the gospel of Christ. At that moment in time, the faith of his mother and grandmother became his faith in Christ. Throughout their years of ministry, Paul built upon those foundations of Timothy's childhood faith. When this letter was written, Timothy was a seasoned believer, but he was apparently struggling to stand firm in his ministry assignment as the pastor of the church at Ephesus. Though separated by miles, Paul continued to encourage Timothy through his letters.

interactive

Below, list the people who have played an important role in your faith journey. Write a note to each of them recalling their influence on your faith and thanking them for encouraging you.

react

Did your parents establish a foundation for your faith in God? How did the faith of your parents become your faith? Why? How are you building faith foundations for your children? How can the community of believers build faith foundations when parents fail to do so?

FROM ONE GENERATION TO ANOTHER

Read Deuteronomy 6:4-9. Timothy's mother and grandmother had followed the directives in this passage: Love God with all your heart, soul, and strength; and teach your children to love God and obey His commandments. Parents have the privilege of establishing the foundations of their children's faith in God by incorporating faith training into every aspect of their days. As you journal below, consider: How is your love for God revealed in your life? What am I doing each day to lead your children to faith in God?

PAUSE to PRAY

Ask God to help you live each day teaching your children to love God. Pray for guidance as you use everyday activities and family routines as ways to share God's love with your children.

The spirit of love overcomes all fears and compels us to serve God.

The Power of Love

2 Tim. 1:6-7

Once Paul reminded Timothy of his spiritual heritage and ministry training, Paul urged him to "fan into flame the gift of God, which is in you through the laying on of my hands." Paul used the image of a waning fire. Since the spark was not extinguished, it could be fanned into a blazing fire. Paul understood Timothy's suffering, but urged him to fulfill his calling by cultivating and using the gift of God. Some believe that God had given Timothy a special gift (from the Greek word charisma) that would be necessary to perform his ministry. Others believe this statement refers to the gift of the Holy Spirit, which is given to all believers. Likewise, the "laying on of my hands" has been interpreted in two different ways. Some claim that the apostle Paul placed his hands on Timothy and literally bestowed the gift of preaching to Timothy. Others feel this action is similar to the ordination services performed in many churches today to symbolize when a person is set apart for specific ministry. Without doubt, Timothy was called and equipped to preach the gospel, a ministry that Paul challenged him to continue.

POWER (DUNAMIS)
Inherent power; capable of accomplishing something. This power resurrected Christ from the dead. The English word "dynamite" is derived from this word.

LOVE (AGAPE)
Used to describe God's unconditional love for humanity, expressed most perfectly in Jesus giving Himself for humanity's redemption.

SELF-DISCIPLINE (SOPHRONISMOS)
The ability to discipline one's mind, to exercise sound judgment, to exercise self-control as a result of having a sound mind.

Aware of Timothy's fearful tendencies, Paul reminded him that God does not give His followers a spirit of timidity (literally a cowardice or terror in difficult situations). Instead God gives a spirit of power, love, and self-discipline. The unconditional love of God, which led Jesus to the cross to secure salvation for everyone who believes in Him, lives within every believer. That Spirit of love is a manifestation of the Holy Spirit. It conquers fear and compels believers to let their love for God shine forth in their lives. Even in the face of adversity and persecution, believers will choose to share God's love with others rather than allow fear to silence their faith. Because People are God's Treasure, God gives His followers the Spirit of love to help them overcome their fears of serving God and sharing the gospel. This Spirit of love urges believers to risk everything so that God's love can be showered on everyone who needs the Savior.

"Nothing will do more to inspire courage, to make a man fearless of danger, or ready to endure privation and persecution, than love. The love of country, and wife, and children, and home, makes the most timid bold when they are assailed; and the love of Christ and of a dying world nerves the soul to great enterprises, and sustains it in the deepest sorrows." Albert Barnes

(http://studylight.org/com/bnn/view.cgi?book=2ti&chapter=1&verse=7#2Ti1_7)

interactive

In the space below, identify some fears that prevent you from living out your faith. Next to each fear, describe how the Spirit of love can overcome that fear.

FEAR   SPIRIT OF LOVE

_____   _____

_____   _____

_____   _____

_____   _____

_____   _____

react

Describe a time when giving in to your fears deprived you of a great experience or blessing. How can our love for God and for people override our fear of living and sharing our faith?

LOVE ONE ANOTHER

Read 1 John 3:21-24. One mark of faith is obedience to God's commands. God has called each of us to "let our light shine" before others. Whenever we feel afraid or intimidated, we only need to ask God for courage and an outpouring of the Spirit of love. As you journal below, consider: How do you respond when fear disrupts your witness of God? How can you confidently live out your faith in a world that seems to be increasingly hostile to Christian witness?

PAUSE to PRAY

Ask God to reveal the fears that prevent you from living out your faith. Pray that you will rely upon the Spirit of love as you share your faith with others.

sealed

conclusion

Because of God's provision, Timothy was well equipped for his ministry calling. His mother and grandmother taught him the Scriptures and prepared Him to accept the gospel. Paul mentored him in the faith. God provided Timothy with the divine gift that he needed. Yet Timothy was still fearful of boldly living his faith. Paul reminded Timothy that he had to choose to rely upon the Spirit of love within him to fulfill his calling. When filled with the Spirit of love, Timothy would no longer be fearful (see 1 John 4:17-18). His love for God and God's love for people would give him the courage to preach the gospel and to remain faithful to Christ. Likewise, when today's believers are timid and afraid, they can rely upon the Spirit of love within them to overcome that fear and boldly live their faith each day.

review

Both Paul and Timothy learned to rely upon the Spirit of love to conquer their fears of living boldly for Christ in spite of potential consequences. By following their example, we can also allow the Spirit to make us faithful witnesses. Why do we allow fear to keep us from sharing the Source of life with people who are dying and going to hell? Why are we intimidated when people ridicule or threaten us instead of determined to honor God with our words and actions? Why do we avoid persecution, when Jesus suffered persecution for us? Why do we fear death, when death ushers us into the presence of God?

COMPELLED BY GOD'S LOVE

Read 1 John 4:7-13. God demonstrated His great love for you by sending His Son to pay for your sins. Whenever you are afraid to let your faith show, either by serving Him or sharing the gospel, you can remember that the Spirit of love—God's great love—now lives inside you. You can choose to let His love flow through you to others. As you journal below, consider: Can you measure the depth of God's love for you? In what ways would God like you to share His love with others?

PAUSE to PRAY

Thank God for His limitless, unconditional love. Pray that you will recognize opportunities to shower that love on others. Thank God for the incredible privilege of serving Him.

16

week 3

the spirit of truth

BIBLICAL PASSAGE: John 14:15-21; 16:12-15

SUPPORTING PASSAGES: John 14:25-27; 16:7-11

MEMORY VERSE: John 16:13

BIBLICAL TRUTH: The Holy Spirit reveals God's truth to us and calls us to obedience.

CONSIDER:

Many cultures embrace an "anything goes" approach to life. People often do whatever seems right in their own eyes, claiming that all choices are acceptable as long as their actions do not significantly hurt others. They hold fast to the belief that truth is relative to an individual's personal situation and deny the concept of absolute truth. Even religious leaders today can disagree on some aspects of biblical truth. With so many voices claiming that truth cannot be clearly defined, how are believers supposed to respond? How can we face the challenge of living by the expressed truths of God's Word in a world that rejects those truths as ancient, out-dated, and irrelevant to today's culture.

Jesus faced similar challenges during His years on earth. The Romans, like the Greeks before them, worshiped a pantheon of gods. The Jewish religious leaders taught obedience to the Law but did not understand or live by the heart of the Law. From this environment, Jesus chose twelve men as His disciples, then invested His time in teaching them God's truths. On the eve of His crucifixion, He assured them that once He departed, the Spirit of truth would continue to reveal God's truths to them. As you study this passage of Scripture, consider these things: How does the Spirit of truth reveal God's Words to believers today? How can your obedience to truth impact an "anything goes" world?

Jesus Prepares the Way

If timing is everything, then Jesus' timing is always perfect. Three times (Matt. 16:21; Matt. 17:12; Matt. 20:18-19), He had tried to tell His disciples what must happen to Him. But they still didn't understand. When Jesus offered these final words of encouragement to His disciples, Judas had departed from the last meal the disciples shared with Jesus. Because Jesus realized that His disciples still didn't understand the necessity of His death, burial, and resurrection, He promised that He would never leave them abandoned and alone. Jesus promised to send Another, One like Him in every way, to be with them to teach and guide them at all times until they could with Him again. Only those who loved Jesus would receive the Spirit and the benefits of unity with the Father and the Son.

sealed

Read John 14:26-29. Jesus prepared His disciples for His death, burial, and resurrection, but He promised they would not have to face those events alone. Through the presence of the Spirit, they would have peace and comfort during the coming storm. As you journal below, consider: What trials has Jesus prepared you to face? Where do you turn during the toughest challenges of your life? How can you experience peace in those storms?

PAUSE to PRAY

Share with God your fears about the events you are facing. Thank Him for giving you the Spirit to comfort you. Pray that you will feel His peace even as the storms rage around you.

Believers demonstrate their love for Christ by obeying His commands.

Signs of Love

2 Tim. 1:3

Jesus challenged His followers to demonstrate their love for Him by obeying His commands. Obedience does not earn salvation or guarantee God's blessings. Obedience is the natural response of a person's internal desire to show great love for another. Within hours, Jesus visibly demonstrated His love for His Father, and for people, by becoming "obedient to death—even death on a cross!" (Phil. 2:8b)

When believers demonstrate their love for God by obeying His commands, they experience God's love in return. The bonds of love between God and His followers provide fertile ground for an intimate relationship. As His people seek Him, God reveals more and more of Himself (see Jer. 29:13). The relationship between God and His followers grows much deeper when both parties are fully invested.

God's love for humanity was expressed through His Son. Jesus' earthly ministry revealed God's love to the disciples who joined Him in ministry and to the people who witnessed the signs and miracles He performed. Earlier in this same conversation, Jesus told Philip: "Anyone who has seen Me has seen the Father" (Jn. 14:9). Through His sacrificial death, Jesus revealed God's love to the world (see Jn. 3:16). God's love for humanity is currently expressed through the indwelling Holy Spirit. Believers are never without God's presence or evidence of His love. His love will be fully revealed when believers dwell with Him for eternity in heaven.

18

react

How do you show love for the people in your life? How can you show love for Jesus? What can happen when your love for Jesus is evident to others?

interactive

As you read through the list below, indicate whether you are motivated by love (L) or a sense of duty (D) to complete these tasks. How does love change an ordinary task into an anticipated pleasure?

___ Study and live by God's Word

___ Love your children

___ Volunteer at kid's schools

___ Spend time in prayer each day

___ Donate food for food bank

___ Provide a meal for a sick friend

___ Take a leadership role at church

___ Get to work on time

___ Attend church on Sunday

___ Host the youth group dinner party

___ Drive the speed limit

___ Vote in local or national elections

___ Pay bills on time

___ Support a mission trip

OBEDIENCE IN LOVE

Read 1 John 2:3-6. John repeated Jesus' call to obedience in these verses. He emphasized that those who know Jesus walk in obedience to His commands. The believer doesn't obey to earn forgiveness or God's favor, Because of their heartfelt devotion to Christ, believers simply desire to imitate Him by walking as He walked. As you journal below, consider: How would you rate your obedience to Christ's commands? What is your motivation for attempting to live as Jesus lived?

Thank God for His love. Ask God to reveal your motives for obeying Christ's commands. Pray that your love for Christ will become the only reason you desire to imitate Him.

Love for other believers provides a *community* where faith is strengthened.

Jesus Promises *the* Spirit

Jn. 14:16-20

Jesus told His disciples that He had to leave them to prepare a place for them in heaven (Jn. 14:1-4). Because He understood that they were distressed by this news, He asked the Father to send "another Counselor" to be with them. This Counselor was given only to those who followed Jesus, never to "the world" who did not believe in Him.

PARAKLETOS

This term is often translated as Counselor or Helper when referring to the Holy Spirit. The Greeks used this word to describe a legal advisor who comes alongside to represent another. When Jesus sent the Counselor to His disciples, He sent an advisor of equal quality, not an inferior substitute. The Holy Spirit always seeks to glorify Jesus while working in His place in the world.

Jesus promised that He wouldn't leave the disciples as orphans who were left alone in the world without a protector and guide. During His post-resurrection appearances, Jesus showed Himself only to those who believed in Him. His presence encouraged His followers to continue the mission He had given to them. These appearances verified His Father's acceptance and promised eternal life for those who followed Him. When the Spirit came upon them, the disciples experienced the fullness of their relationship with the triune God that enabled them to proclaim the gospel with boldness.

Believers today experience the same unity with Jesus through the presence of the Holy Spirit. Jesus had personally revealed God's truths to His disciples. The Spirit of truth reveals the fullness of God's truth to present-day believers. Jesus walked with His disciples, guiding them, comforting them, and providing for their needs. Believers can rely upon the Holy Spirit to be their Guide, Comforter, and Provider.

react

When believers feel abandoned, how can the Spirit of truth reassure them of God's love? How does the presence of the Spirit guarantee that believers will spend eternity in heaven? How does the Spirit of truth offer guidance and comfort to Jesus' followers?

FILLED WITH THE SPIRIT

Read Titus 3:4-8. Jesus saves those who believe in Him by washing away (forgiving) their sins, granting them new life (spiritual rebirth) through the Spirit, and guaranteeing them eternal life. Filled with the Spirit, believers then devote themselves to doing what is good. As you journal below, consider: When did you receive forgiveness for your sins? How can you be certain that you will experience eternal life? How does the Spirit's presence inspire you to do what is good and pleasing to God?

PAUSE to PRAY

If you have any doubts about salvation, confess Jesus as your Savior and receive the gift of eternal life. Thank God for the Spirit's presence in your life. Commit to following Jesus wholeheartedly.

The spirit of love overcomes all fears and compels us to serve God.

The Power of Love

2 Tim. 1:6-7

Jesus realized that His disciples were overwhelmed with everything He had told them thus far, and yet He still had much more to share with them. He explained that the Spirit of truth would continue to reveal God's truths when the disciples were ready to hear them. Jesus assured His followers that they could fully trust the Spirit to speak only the truths that He heard from God. The Spirit of truth would glorify Jesus by sharing with the disciples everything the Father had made known to Jesus.

After Jesus ascended into heaven, the Spirit of truth guided the disciples as they spread the gospel and started churches throughout the world. Because The Bible is God's Word, the Spirit of truth ensured that the Bible correctly revealed God's commands. Under the power of the Spirit, the apostles recorded the events of Jesus' ministry (the Gospels), the beginning of the church (Acts), the theology and practice of the Christian faith (the Epistles), and the prophecies concerning future events (Revelation). Peter testified that the Spirit inspired men to record the prophecies contained in Scripture (2 Peter 1:20-21). Paul emphasized that all Scripture is God-breathed and provides instruction for believers (2 Tim. 3:16).

The Spirit of truth continues to reveal Jesus to believers by convicting persons of their sin, leading them to place their faith in Christ, and teaching them God's truths through the Scriptures. By making God's commands known to believers, the Spirit also calls them to obedience. Believers can fully rely upon the revelation of the Spirit because the Spirit always leads them to greater understanding of the character, mission, and calling of Christ.

"Our Lord was always careful to give His disciples the right amount of truth at the best time for them to receive it. The Holy Spirit is our Teacher today, and He follows that same principle: He teaches us the truths we need to know, when we need them and when we are ready to receive them." Warren W. Wiersbe

interactive

In the space provided below, list five challenging issues in your life. How often (F—frequently; S—sometimes; R—rarely) do you rely upon the Spirit of truth to guide you as you make decisions in these areas? If you surrendered these concerns to the Spirit, how would He tell you to handle them?

____ Issue 1: _____

____ Issue 2: _____

____ Issue 3: _____

____ Issue 4: _____

____ Issue 5: _____

react

Describe a time when the Spirit revealed new truths to you through a familiar passage of Scripture or helped you to understand a difficult passage. How did the Spirit use those truths to minister to your needs?

SPIRIT INSPIRED SCRIPTURES

Read 2 Peter 1:16-21. Peter assured his readers that the disciples weren't repeating fantastic stories. They had witnessed Christ's transfiguration on the mountain and had heard God declare His love for His Son. The words of the prophets, inspired by the Spirit, had been fulfilled in their presence. As you journal below, consider: Are you confident that the Scriptures are the inspired Word of God? Do you allow the Spirit of truth to reveal how God's Word applies to the specific circumstances of your life?

PAUSE to PRAY

Thank God for the Spirit's role in preserving God's Words for your instruction. Before reading the Bible each day, ask the Spirit to reveal the fullness of Scripture to you.

Truth Given to Believers

The Spirit of truth is God's presence in the world today. The Spirit guided the first-century disciples when they preached the gospel, planted churches, and wrote letters that became the books of the New Testament. The Spirit reveals the righteousness of Christ to the world and convicts people of their sins. When believers study the Bible, the Spirit of truth enables believers to understand God's Word. At times, the Spirit of truth may give believers specific verses to apply to situations they face. Sometimes, the Spirit speaks to believers through prayer or through the counsel of other Christians. The Spirit of truth enables believers to apply God's Words to their lives so they can walk in full obedience to Jesus' commands.

review

Jesus promised that the Spirit of truth will continue to reveal God's truths to His followers while serving as their Teacher, Counselor, and Comforter. How does the Spirit serve as a Teacher in your walk with Christ? When has the Spirit offered counseling for the difficult situations in your life? When have you felt the comforting presence of the Spirit as you struggled to face unpleasant circumstances? How would you explain to others the ways that the Spirit of truth promotes spiritual growth in your life?

CONTINUE ON

Read 2 Timothy 3:14-17. Paul urged Timothy, a fellow servant of Christ, to continue spreading the gospel and following the teachings of Scripture. The faith he had learned from the Scriptures led to salvation and wisdom. He could rely on the truths of the Word as he taught new believers, corrected those who strayed, and urged all believers to greater righteousness. As you journal below, consider: What authority does Scripture have in your life? How does obedience to God's commands equip you for life's challenges?

PAUSE to PRAY

Thank God for revealing His wisdom through Scripture. Pray that the Spirit will help you use God's Word as you teach, correct, and strengthen others in the faith.

24

week 4
the spirit of life

BIBLICAL PASSAGE: Romans 8:1-4, 12-17

SUPPORTING PASSAGES: Romans 8:5-11; Galatians 5:16-26

MEMORY VERSE: Romans 8:2

BIBLICAL TRUTH: The Holy Spirit brings life by defeating the power of sin in our lives.

CONSIDER

The Spirit of truth reveals the commands which believers are called to obey. Believers understand that all sinful behavior, whether mild or severe in human eyes, stands between them and God. Yet they often struggle to live according to God's commands. Just when they think they have conquered a sinful habit, they find themselves trapped in that pattern of behavior. They confess the sin, ask forgiveness, pick themselves up and dust themselves off, and then march forward in new determination to obey. Maybe a week goes by, maybe six months. Then one day, without warning, they find themselves caught once again in that sinful behavior. Do you recognize a similar struggle in your life? Are you feeling defeated? Would you like to discover how to defeat the power of sin in your life?

Jesus proclaimed, "The thief comes only to steal and kill and destroy; I have come that they may have life, and have it to the full" (John 10:10). Jesus revealed that Satan works to destroy humanity's relationship with Him, but that He has won the battle. Jesus promised His followers life, abundant life that far exceeds their expectations, through the power of the Spirit of life.

Understanding the Battle

The apostle Paul experienced this struggle against sin. He lamented, "I do not understand what I do. For what I want to do I do not do, but what I hate I do" (Rom. 7:15). He longed to do what God expected of him, and yet committed the very acts he wanted to avoid. Paul described the battle that all Christians face—the battle between the flesh and the Spirit. The flesh refers to the sinful condition of people prior to salvation. Even after salvation, the desires of the flesh continue to oppose the desires of the Spirit. When believers follow the desires of the flesh, they sin against God. But when they allow the Spirit of life to guide their choices, believers discover that the desires of the flesh can be defeated.

Read John 5:24, 39-40; 14:6; and 20:31. The apostle John recorded many times that Jesus told His followers how to find eternal life. Jesus emphasized that only those people who hear the Word and believe in Him will receive life; they are no longer condemned for their sins. As you journal below, consider: When did you recognize Jesus as the only way to eternal life? How has His assurance that your sins are forgiven changed the way you live each day? Are you regularly sharing this message of hope with others?

PAUSE to PRAY

Thank God for eternal life found in His Son, Jesus Christ. Ask God to show you others who are desperate to find new life in Him. Pray for boldness to share Christ with others.

Believers are set free from the bondage of sin by the Spirit of life.

Signs of Love

Romans 8:1-4

By beginning with the word, "therefore," Paul tied the content of this chapter with the previous ones. In chapters 3-7, Paul described the human dilemma—all people have sinned and fallen short of the glory of God (Rom. 3:23), and all people will be condemned or sentenced to death for their sins (see Rom. 5:12 and 6:23a). He emphasized that the only way people can be justified, or made right with God, is by receiving salvation through faith in Jesus Christ (see Rom. 4:24-25; 5:6-9; and 6:23b). For this reason, those who accept Jesus as Savior will not suffer condemnation. The Spirit of life has set believers free—free from the penalty of death and free from the sinful desires of the flesh. Through the Spirit of life, believers are promised eternal life in heaven as well as the abundant life on earth that Jesus promised His followers.

JUSTIFIED (DIKAIOO)
A person is justified, or restored to a right relationship with God, through the crucifixion and resurrection of Jesus. To allow people to be forgiven and made "just" in God's eyes, Jesus presented Himself as a perfect sacrifice and died on the cross. God declares those who place their faith in Christ as righteous or justified before Him.

Jesus came to earth "in the likeness of sinful man" to fulfill the requirements of the law, something no other human could do. Through His sinless life, which was marked by complete obedience to God's commands (see 2 Cor. 5:21 and Heb. 4:15), Jesus defeated the power of sin by offering Himself as the perfect sacrifice. He "condemned sin in sinful man" by defeating death and by breaking the power of sin in the lives of His followers. When His work on earth was finished and He returned to His Father in heaven, He sent the Holy Spirit to His followers. The Spirit of life brings new life to believers through spiritual rebirth. The Spirit of life brings abundant life by enabling believers to defeat the bonds of sin so they might live in a manner pleasing to God. The Spirit of life guarantees eternal life for those who place their faith in Christ.

Why was it important for Jesus, in human likeness, to fully obey the law and defeat the power of sin and death? How has the Spirit of life been manifested in your life? How does the Spirit empower you to set aside the desires of the flesh and walk righteously before God?

FROM LAW TO LIFE

Read Galatians 3:22-25. According to Scripture, every person is a prisoner to sin, is unable to keep God's commandments, and desperately needs a Savior. The Bible reveals humanity's sinful nature and the way of salvation. When people accept Christ as Savior, their sins are forgiven and they are given eternal life. As you journal below, consider: How did the Bible reveal your inability to earn God's favor? What does forgiveness mean to you?

Thank God for the Scriptures that led you to Him. Celebrate the freedom from condemnation that is yours through faith in Christ.

Believers are called to submit to the *guidance* of the Spirit.

A *New* Obligation

Romans 8:12-14

Because Christ paid the debt for sin and now lives within believers (vv. 5-11), Christians have a new and surpassing obligation. Believers are no longer compelled to respond to the desires of the flesh which is a choice that leads to death. Instead, they are obligated to walk in obedience to the Spirit of life. Although believers receive forgiveness and new life in Christ, they soon discover that the sinful desires of their former (unsaved) lives still exist. Whenever the flesh appeals to them, Christians must resist those appeals and determine "to live self-controlled, upright and godly lives" (Titus 2:12). Believers will find that they are incapable, under their own strength, of resisting the sinful desires. However, the Spirit of life gives them the power to defeat the desires of the flesh.

Paul challenged believers to recognize evil as evil and to intentionally "put to death" their evil desires. This process of mortification, a term used by theologians, requires the believer to actively "crucify" any evil desires instead of passively waiting until Jesus or the Holy Spirit subdues those desires for them. The only way that believers can meet this challenge is to rely upon the Sprit of life to guide their responses. Believers who decide to walk in the Spirit demonstrate their new identity as children of God, for only the saved possess the Spirit. As believers strengthen their obedience to the Spirit, they become more and more like Christ and find themselves living the abundant life that Jesus promised to His followers.

react

How would you define the sinful nature and the misdeeds of the body? Why do you think that Christians continue to struggle against the desires of the flesh? What must a believer do to conquer those desires each day?

interactive

The list below mentions several areas in which believers might struggle between the desires of the flesh versus the guidance of the Spirit. Identify any struggles you have in these areas. Pray that you will follow the Spirit and "put to death" the desires of the flesh.

Financial matters _____

Career guidance _____

Parenting _____

Leisure activities _____

Spiritual growth _____

Politics _____

Assisting aging parents _____

Personal health _____

Friendships _____

Retirement planning _____

FIGHTING THE BATTLE

Read Galatians 5:16-17 and 22-25. Paul explained that believers must choose to follow the Spirit instead of allowing their sinful desires to lead them astray. Thankfully, the Spirit gives believers the strength necessary to deny those desires. When believers walk in the Spirit, He produces fruit in their lives that marks them as followers of Christ. As you journal below, consider: How frequently do you experience the battle between flesh and Spirit? How does your life exhibit the fruit of the Spirit?

PAUSE to PRAY

Pray for the desire to walk with the Spirit each day. Thank God that He is producing fruit in your life in keeping with His character. Ask for opportunities to serve others in His name.

Through the presence of the Spirit, believers are declared *children* of God.

Adopted *by* God

Romans 8:15-17

People who place their faith in Christ are no longer slaves to fear—the fears that consume those who do not believe in Christ. People without Christ fear God because they cannot live up to the standards He has established. They worry because they can never be good enough to earn God's favor. They realize that even their best efforts will result in condemnation and death. Just as slaves frequently tremble fearfully before their masters, those who do not believe in Christ often fear death and God's judgment.

Because they have placed their faith in Christ, believers experience an entirely new relationship with God. This relationship is marked by intimacy and acceptance; fear is forever banished. Because God adopts believers as His children, their ties to their old ways of life are permanently severed; they become full heirs of the kingdom of God. The Spirit of life seals or guarantees their redemption and future inheritance (Eph. 1:13-14). Believers then enjoy the privilege of addressing God as "Abba, Father," an intimate phrase similar to children addressing their earthly fathers as "Daddy," or "Papa."

When believers allow the Spirit of life to guide their actions, they begin to reflect the character of Christ and live according to His teachings. This outward demonstration of their faith does not necessarily win them favor in this world. Many believers will "share in His sufferings" because the world ridicules or persecutes them for their belief in Christ (see John 15:18-19). Believers who remain steadfastly committed to Christ through suffering and persecution demonstrate their new life in Christ. As a result, they will share in His glory as well—they will live eternally in His presence.

"The term adoption itself implies the act of taking officially the child of another to be one's own. This is what God does as the result of the finished work of the Cross. Through grace He takes a child of the devil and makes him His son, and the Spirit certifies the sonship. In Paul's use of the term, there is the contrast between the Spirit of Adoption—permanent security; and the spirit of bondage—the temporary relationship of slave to master." Herbert Lockyer (p. 314-315).

interactive

List characteristics of a perfect father below. Why are these characteristics important to you?

_____   _____
_____   _____
_____   _____
_____   _____

How does your relationship with your earthly father influence your understanding of God as your heavenly Father? What benefits do you enjoy as a child of God?

ADOPTED BY GOD

Read Galatians 4:3-7. According to God's plan, Jesus is the Redeemer of humanity. When people accept His gift of salvation, they are adopted into God's family and receive all rights promised to His children. This new relationship is reflected in the privilege of calling God "Abba, Father." As you journal below, consider: Do you see God as a distant and judgmental deity or as your heavenly Father? What does it mean to you to be adopted as His child? Do you live to please Him or to please yourself or other people?

PAUSE to PRAY

Thank God for adopting you as His child. Pray that you will understand how to approach Him as a Father who loves you greatly. Consider how you might introduce others to your Father.

People who place their faith in Jesus Christ receive forgiveness of their sins and the joy of a restored relationship with God. At the moment of their confession of faith, the Spirit of life grants them new spiritual life in Christ, equips them to ignore the desires of the flesh and walk according to God's commands, and guarantees them eternal life. This same Spirit testifies to their new relationship with God—they are adopted into God's family and become co-heirs with Christ in the kingdom of God. As the recipients of so many blessings, believers are obligated to live righteously before God by deliberately ignoring the temptations of the flesh and calling upon the power of the Spirit to guide them through each day.

review

From new life, to daily life, to eternal life, the Spirit of life makes abundant life possible for those who place their faith in Christ. How would you describe your life before you met Christ? How has your life changed since you accepted Christ as your Savior? How does the Spirit help you defeat the temptations of the flesh so that you can honor Christ through your actions each day? How does the assurance of eternal life help you to withstand ridicule or persecution for your faith?

A WORTHY INHERITANCE

Read 1 Peter 1:3-7. Scripture promises that all who believe in Christ share an inheritance that cannot perish, spoil, or fade—eternal life. Until that inheritance can be claimed, believers may suffer all kinds of trails for their faith. Even in suffering, faithful believers bring glory and honor to Christ. As you journal below, consider: How have you responded when people ridiculed your faith? Did you response ease your suffering or bring glory and honor to Christ? How will you choose to respond to future trials of faith?

PAUSE to PRAY

Pray that your actions will honor Christ at all times, but especially when you must suffer for your faith. Thank God for an inheritance worthy of suffering.

week 5

the spirit of wisdom & revelation

BIBLICAL PASSAGE: Ephesians 1:17-19a; 1 Corinthians 2:9-13

SUPPORTING PASSAGES: Galatians 5:5-6; Ephesians 3:2-12; 1 Corinthians 2:6-16

MEMORY VERSE: Ephesians 1:17

BIBLICAL TRUTH: The Holy Spirit reveals the full wisdom of God to believers.

CONSIDER

What do you admire most about some of the Christians in your life? Perhaps they seem to have a "best friend" connection with God. Maybe they are living life with the assurance of a God-given purpose and vision. Perhaps they peacefully endure hardships that would break others because they know this life is temporary and a great reward awaits them in heaven. Maybe they are the people that others seek for wisdom and guidance to deal with puzzling or complicated life circumstances. Believers who are seeking this intimate relationship with God can trust the Spirit of wisdom and revelation to help them achieve it.

The Damascus Road encounter with Christ was simply the beginning of Paul's life-long journey with God. As the Spirit of wisdom and revelation worked in Paul's life, he developed an intimate relationship with God that he wanted all believers to experience for themselves. As you complete this lesson, consider these questions: Is your knowledge of God limited to what you read about Him in the Bible? Or do you have an intimate relationship with Him that allows you to hear His voice and receive spiritual truths from Him? What purpose does God have for your life? Are you living with those purposes in mind, even through difficult times, because you know that heaven awaits you?

Sealed by the Spirit

Paul began the letter to the church at Ephesus by celebrating God's gift of salvation through Jesus Christ. He emphasized that God's plan for reconciling people to Him had been accomplished through the sacrifice of His Son. Because of God's lavish grace, believers receive redemption and forgiveness for their sins through Christ's shed blood. And God's grace extends far beyond salvation. God gives spiritual wisdom and understanding to His followers so that they might know His will—His plan "to bring all things in heaven and on earth together under one head, even Christ" (Eph. 1:10). Furthermore, believers are marked or sealed with the Holy Spirit as a guarantee that God will fulfill His promise to provide an inheritance—the gift of eternal life.

Read 1 Peter 1:3-5. When Peter wrote to the believers in Asia Minor, he praised God for giving them salvation through their faith in Jesus Christ. He reminded the believers that God's purposes had been accomplished through Jesus' sacrifice—to give believers a living hope and the promise of eternal life. Shielded by God's power on earth, believers will one day dwell with God in heaven. As you journal below, consider: What does God's mercy mean to you? How does the assurance of your inheritance provide hope during the days you spend on earth?

PAUSE to PRAY

Express your gratitude to God for His plan to bring you into His kingdom. Thank Him for the inheritance He has guaranteed you.

We can rely upon the Spirit of wisdom and revelation to understand the fulness of God's *character, blessings,* and *power*.

The Spirit Reveals God

Eph. 1:17-19a

Paul prayed that the Spirit of wisdom and revelation would reveal the fullness of God to His followers. As the Spirit continued to give them greater understanding of God's character and majesty, they would know Him better. Through this intimate knowledge of God, believers would be drawn into a deeply personal relationship with Him. In these verses, Paul prayed that the "eyes of their hearts may be enlightened." In biblical language, the heart refers to an individual's physical, mental, intellectual, and spiritual life. When the believer's heart is open, the Spirit can reveal everything that God has made available to His followers.

First, believers receive a calling from God, which has past, present, and future significance. At some point in the past, believers received salvation. During the remaining years of life, they live with God's calling to direct the actions of their lives. Finally, believers "know the hope" of eternal life. This hope is not merely human wishful thinking; this hope is the firm assurance that God will bring His promise to fruition.

Second, believers will receive "the riches of his glorious inheritance in the saints." Just as God raised Christ from the dead, He promises to raise believers from the dead. They will enjoy eternal rest and peace in heaven in the presence of God. Third, this feat will be accomplished through the "incomparably great power" of God—the power God exerted when He resurrected Christ. In the verses that follow, Paul used every adjective he could to describe God's great and unequalled power.

34

WISDOM (SOPHIA)

Knowledge, insight, and a deep understanding of spiritual matters revealed by God to His followers. Wisdom provides believers with the ability to sustain their relationship with God by managing their affairs using good judgment and divine guidance.

REVELATION (APOKALUPSIS)

This terms describes the act of revealing, disclosing, or unveiling spiritual truths while also providing proper interpretation. In this verse, the Spirit fully understands the deep things of God and reveals and explains those things to believers.

"We can know about God, but we can only know Him in all the glory of His personality as He reveals Himself to us. He has revealed Himself in two ways—in the inspired Word and the incarnate Word. He has said what He is like in the one, and He has shown what He is like in the other." – John Phillips

respond

How would you describe the difference between knowledge and wisdom? Why must the Spirit reveal spiritual truths to believers? How would you define the hope that Christians have in Christ?

WISDOM'S PURPOSE

Read Colossians 1:9-12. Paul prayed that believers would be given spiritual wisdom and understanding so they could know God's will. By living according to the will of God, believers would be strengthened to bear fruit in their work for the kingdom. As you journal below, consider: Do you find it difficult to discern God's will? How does understanding God's will strengthen your service for Him? Is your faith pleasing to God? Does your work for His kingdom reflect the worth of your salvation?

Ask God to reveal His will for your life as you read the Bible and pray for His guidance.
Thank God for your salvation and commit yourself to living in ways that please Him.

We can rely upon the Spirit to reveal the things God has *prepared* for us.

The Spirit *Reveals* God's work

1 Cor. 2:9-10

In his first letter to the church at Corinth, Paul described the work of the Spirit of wisdom and revelation in greater detail. Paul explained that the wisdom of God was not available to everyone, but only to those who believed in Christ and received the Spirit. To substantiate this statement, Paul quoted from Isaiah 64:4. Prior to salvation, the human mind cannot hear, see, or comprehend the blessings that God has prepared for His followers.

Many of the Greeks placed a high value on gaining knowledge and engaging in philosophical debate. Despite their knowledge, the secret wisdom of God was hidden from them. They could not understand the simple message of the Gospel—that Jesus, God's Son, offered Himself as the atoning sacrifice for sin so that people could be reconciled to God. Through the Spirit of wisdom and revelation, God chose to reveal this message to people who confessed their faith in Christ. The Spirit searches out the "deep things of God" and shares those spiritual truths with all believers.

interactive

Read the verses listed below to discover some of the things God has prepared for us.

Jeremiah 29:11-13 _____

Philippians 1:6 _____

Ephesians 2:8-10 _____

Romans 12:1-2 _____

John 14:1-4 _____

Revelation 21:1-4 _____

react

Prior to placing your faith in Christ, did God's plan for salvation make sense to you? When you share the gospel with others, do you sense their struggle to understand God's plan? How can the Spirit of wisdom and revelation guide your efforts to explain spiritual truths to believers and seekers?

SEEK WISDOM & UNDERSTANDING

Read Proverbs 2:1-6. King Solomon used six descriptive phrases when he commanded his son to seek diligently for wisdom, discernment, and understanding. His message remains important for today's believers—search for wisdom as you would seek hidden treasure and you will receive wisdom, knowledge and understanding from God. As you journal below, consider: Is wisdom a treasure that you seek? How diligently do you search for it? Do you hoard the treasures that God reveals or share them with others?

PAUSE to PRAY

Thank God that He gives wisdom and understanding to us. Ask Him to reveal wisdom for the challenges that you face. Pray that you will be able to share His wisdom with others.

We can rely upon the Spirit to reveal God's wisdom through *spiritual truths.*

The Spirit *Reveals* God's Truths

1 Cor. 2:11-13

Paul pointed out that one person cannot know the private thoughts and feelings of another. Similarly, mere humans cannot comprehend God's thoughts. As the third person of the Trinity (God the Father, Jesus the Son, and the Holy Spirit), the Spirit is God and intimately "knows the thoughts of God." Because **The Holy Spirit is God and Empowerer,** He reveals to believers the deep things of God and uses those spiritual truths to bring meaning and purpose to their lives.

Paul continued to emphasize the distinction between the wisdom of God revealed to believers and the wisdom of the world. In this context, the "spirit of the world" does not refer to Satan, but to the accumulation of worldly wisdom based on human effort and reasoning (see 1 Cor. 1:20; 2:6; and 3:19). Believers are no longer bound by the conventions of human wisdom which is foolishness before God. Believers, through the Spirit of wisdom and revelation, now have the mind of Christ.

The philosophers and learned men of Corinth often criticized and/or ridiculed Paul's simple message. But Paul was neither discouraged nor beaten. Instead, Paul reminded his critics that the words he spoke were "taught by the Spirit," and revealed spiritual truths to those with spiritual ears to hear them. He further explained that people without the Spirit cannot understand or accept spiritual truths. As believers continue to preach the gospel and share spiritual truths for daily living, they must be careful to speak only the words that the Spirit gives them.

interactive

Complete the following chart by comparing worldly wisdom versus the wisdom of God. (See examples.) Why doesn't God's wisdom make sense to those who don't have a relationship with God?

WORLDLY WISDOM	GOD'S WISDOM
Hate your enemies	Love your enemies
Get even with people who torment you	Pray for people who persecute you
Accumulate money & material possessions	
Keep up with the latest gossip at work	
Pad the expense account when traveling	
Let children & teens set their own schedules	

38

respond

Which is easier to live by: the world's wisdom or God's wisdom? Describe a time when relying upon godly wisdom brought peace and healing to a painful situation. Why should Christians rely upon the Spirit of wisdom when sharing Christ or offering counsel to others?

TRUST GOD'S WAYS

Read Isaiah 55:8-11. God clearly declares that His thoughts and ways are higher than our thoughts and ways, a strong reminder that He is God and we are not. He promises that His Word will always achieve its purpose and accomplish His desires. We can trust in the power of His Word to give us wisdom for daily living as well as difficult times. As you journal below, consider: Have you learned to trust God's thoughts and ways instead of relying your own ideas? How has His Word given purpose to your life? What has His Word accomplished in your life?

PAUSE to PRAY

Ask God to help you trust His ways instead of your own. Pray that His purposes will be accomplished in your life as you trust His Word.

The gift of salvation is only the beginning of God's provision for His followers. God desires an intimate personal relationship with every believer, so He chooses to reveal Himself, His works, and His truths through the Spirit of wisdom and revelation. As believers grow in their understanding of God and live in daily communion with Him, they will learn to trust in God's wisdom instead of relying upon the foolish wisdom of this world. Believers will allow the Spirit of wisdom and revelation to guide their words and actions as they share Christ and spiritual truths with others. Encouraged by the certain hope of spending eternity in heaven, believers will spend their time on earth preparing themselves and others for that day.

review

Without the assistance of the Spirit of wisdom and revelation, believers would not be able to know God or understand spiritual truths. How does the certain hope of eternity in heaven bring purpose and meaning to your life? What do you think God has planned for your life? What new spiritual truths have you learned through this study? How will the Spirit use those truths in your life? Which people in your lives might also need to hear these truths? How can the Spirit help you communicate those truths through words and/or actions?

PRAY FOR WISDOM

Read James 1:5-8. James urged believers to ask God to supply the wisdom necessary for living a life of faith. God generously supplies the wisdom believers need; believers must be ready to act on that wisdom. When believers second-guess God's wisdom, they reveal their doubts and will fail to recognize and follow His counsel. As you journal below, consider: Do you turn to God for wisdom to deal with life's challenges? How do you respond when God's wisdom matches your understanding of the situation? How do you respond when His guidance doesn't seem to make sense?

PAUSE to PRAY

Thank God that He generously gives wisdom for every situation you face. Ask Him to guide your decisions each day. Pray that you will always act on His guidance.

week 6
spirit of glory

BIBLICAL PASSAGE: 1 Peter 4:7-14

SUPPORTING PASSAGES: Matthew 5:11-12; John 15:18-27; Romans 12:3-8; 1 Corinthians 12:1-20; 13:4-7; Hebrews 13:1-2; 1 Peter 4:15-19

MEMORY VERSE: 1 Peter 4:14

BIBLICAL TRUTH: The Holy Spirit dwells within us so we may ultimately bring glory to God.

Christians are called to live so that God is glorified in every word and deed; yet few believers consistently achieve this purpose. Many believers, no matter how hard they try, find themselves acting in ways that prove their inability to glorify God through their own efforts. And when they do manage to bring glory to God, they may suffer ridicule, hate, or even stronger forms of persecution for their faith. Although they mentally acknowledge that believers sometimes suffer for their faith, they are often stunned when persecution strikes them personally. Through these experiences, believers begin to understand the necessity of relying upon the Spirit of glory for the ability to see God's glory and reflect His glory to others. As you complete this study, consider: How can believers glorify God in their daily lives? Why should believers be willing to suffer for their faith—and how is God glorified through their suffering? How does the Spirit of glory strengthen believers who face persecution for their faith?

Through his life experiences, the apostle Peter learned that bringing glory to God in his own strength was virtually impossible. In contrast, when he relied on the Spirit, his words and deeds glorified God. As Jesus had warned, his faithfulness to Christ brought persecution and suffering. In those circumstances, Peter learned to rely upon the Spirit of glory to give him strength to endure—and even rejoice—in suffering

A Powerful Witness

The apostle Peter was a walking testimony of the power of the Spirit in the life of a believer. On the eve of Jesus' crucifixion, despite his claim that he would die for Christ, Peter denied Christ three times (Mark 14:66-72). After His resurrection from the dead, Jesus restored Peter and challenged him to feed and care for His sheep. Jesus did not hesitate to tell Peter that serving Him would cost his life (John 21:15-19). Once filled with the Spirit at Pentecost, Peter found strength to fulfill Jesus' calling despite significant personal cost. As Peter led the disciples in preaching the gospel and establishing churches, he frequently suffered hardship, persecution, and even imprisonment. According to church tradition, when Nero condemned Peter to death for his faith, Peter chose to be crucified upside down. Through loving others, serving Christ, and suffering for his faith, Peter knew the power of the Spirit of glory.

sealed

A LIFE THAT GLORIFIES GOD

Read Matthew 5:13-16. Jesus challenged His disciples to live their faith before all people each day. He compared their Christian actions to salt and light—unmistakable signs of their commitment to Him that could change the world around them. Jesus said the good deeds of believers bring glory to God. As you journal below, consider: Are your words and actions seasoned with God's love? Does your faith shine brightly before the people around you? How does your faithfulness bring glory to God?

PAUSE to PRAY

Ask God to fill you with His Spirit so that your words and deeds reveal Him to the world. Pray that others will want to know God because they have witnessed your faith in Him in action.

By walking in the Spirit, believers reveal God's glory through their *love* for others.

Called to Love
Eph. 1:17-19a

Peter challenged fellow Christians to live their lives in full service to God because they would be held accountable for their actions (1 Pet. 4:1-5). By reminding fellow believers that "the end of all things is near," Peter emphasized the importance of devoted Christian living. He urged Christians to remain "clear minded and self-controlled," so they could recognize and pray for the needs of individuals and the church in the final days. With their minds clearly focused on their mission, believers wouldn't become so excited about Christ's return that they neglected the duties of Christian witness (see 1 Thes. 4:11 and 2 Thes. 2:2). By praying continually about their circumstances and their mission, Christ's followers would receive clear directions from God for their important work.

Peter emphasized the importance of loving each other deeply. The Greek word, agape, describes God's unconditional love for humanity as well as the love that believers are called to show others. When practicing agape love, believers often put the needs of others before their own, even the needs of enemies or those who have hurt them. Peter explained that agape love "covers over a multitude of sins." While believers cannot condone or cover up sin, they can choose to forgive others because Christ first forgave them. Instead of seeking retaliation or exposing others' sins, believers can encourage repentance and reconciliation by practicing agape love.

In the first century church, believers were encouraged to show hospitality to traveling Christians and ministers of the gospel because hotels and restaurants were virtually non-existent. Although this ministry could strain a family's resources, believers were urged to share with warmth and compassion instead of grumbling or complaining. By showing agape love for others, which is only possible when people rely on the Spirit, Christians reveal God's glory to the world.

42

respond

How does prayer for the circumstances of believers and the church keep us focused on the mission of revealing God's glory to a watching world? How does forgiveness overcome sin without condoning it? What are some ways for believers to practice hospitality today?

SHARING GOD'S LOVE

Read Romans 5:5-10. Jesus loved us enough to die for us, even while we were still His enemies. When we become Christians, God pours His love into us through the indwelling Spirit. As followers of Christ, we have the ability to share His love with others so that they might also be reconciled to Him. As you journal below, consider: How has God's love changed your life? Do you share God's love with others—including your enemies—by loving them, forgiving them, and showing hospitality to them?

PAUSE to PRAY

Thank God for loving you. Ask God to show you where you have withheld His love from others. Pray that His love will flow through you to others, even to your enemies.

sealed

Gifted to Serve

1 Pet. 4:10-11

Through the Spirit, every Christian has received one or more spiritual gifts. As good stewards of God's gifts, believers are expected to exercise those gifts in ministry to fellow believers and to draw others into the kingdom of God. By "faithfully administering God's grace," Christians become vital partners with God in His work on earth. When believers understand and appreciate their gifts and the gifts of others, they will work together to form the living body of Christ. Because **The Church is God's Plan** for establishing the kingdom of God, she will excel at her mission to make disciples and teach them to obey all that Christ has commanded (see Matt. 28:19-20).

Peter emphasized two categories of spiritual gifts—speaking gifts and serving gifts. By comparing this passage with Romans 12:6-8 and 1 Corinthians 12:4-11, believers can see how the different gifts might fit into these categories. Believers who claim to speak for God, whether professional ministers or simply good friends offering godly counsel, are challenged to speak "the very words of God." Likewise, believers who minister through such gifts as giving, showing mercy, offering leadership, or serving others are encouraged to perform those tasks "with the strength God provides." All gifts should be used to bring glory and praise to God, who gave the gifts, not to benefit the individual believer. When all believers use their gifts in concert, under the guidance of the Spirit, the church becomes a powerful witness that reveals God's glory to the world.

Spiritual Gifts are the specific gifts or talents given by the Holy Spirit to believers at the moment of their salvation. Using these gifts, believers are equipped to participate fully in the ministry of the church by spreading the gospel and strengthening the faith of believers. Believers should not use these gifts for their own benefits or claim that certain gifts are better than others. Rather believers should serve the church in an effort to reveal God's glory to the world. (For a deeper study of spiritual gifts, see Rom. 12:3-8, 1 Cor. 12:1-11; and Eph. 4:11-16.)

interactive

Romans 12:6-8 offers a partial listing of spiritual gifts. Beside each gift, list ways Christians can use that gift to serve the church and bring glory to God. Draw a star next to the gift(s) that God has given you.

Prophesying _____

Teaching _____

Giving _____

Showing Mercy _____

Serving _____

Encouraging _____

Leading _____

44

respond

Why are all gifts necessary for the church to fulfill its mission to make and teach disciples? How are spiritual gifts used to strengthen the ministries of your church?

USE YOUR GIFTS

Read Ephesians 4:11-13. Paul described various ways that spiritual gifts can be used within the body of Christ. Regardless of the ways God uses your gifts, His goal is to equip all of His children for works of service. As believers use their gifts to build up the church, every member will reach spiritual maturity by knowing God and becoming more like Christ. As you journal below, consider: Have you identified your spiritual gifts? Are you using those gifts to serve the body of Christ? Are the people of your church growing in their relationship with God and becoming more like Christ?

PAUSE to PRAY

Thank God for the gifts that He has given to you. Ask Him to show you how He wants to use those gifts to build up the faith of others.

A *Glimpse* of Glory

1 Pet. 4:12-14

When believers show God's love to all people and serve Him in ministry, they are separated from those who do not honor God. As a result, believers should not be surprised when they face painful trials and suffering. The Greek word for "painful" means "burning" and refers to the refining that takes place when metals are purified. Peter encouraged believers to accept suffering as a method for refining their faith and participating "in the sufferings of Christ." Perhaps Peter remembered Jesus' warning: "If they persecuted me, they will persecute you also" (John 15:20b). Peter promised that Christ's glory is revealed when His servants suffer. The apostle Paul echoed his words. As children of God and co-heirs with Christ, believers will suffer, but that temporary suffering will not compare to the glory that will be revealed in them (see Rom. 8:17-18).

Jesus warned His followers: "Blessed are you when people insult you, persecute you and falsely say all kinds of evil against you because of me. Rejoice and be glad, because great is your reward in heaven" (Matt. 5:11-12b). When believers are persecuted for their faith, "the Spirit of glory and of God rests" upon them. In these circumstances, believers may be given glimpses of God's glory and their future with Him. Strengthened by these visions, which may be revealed through reading Scripture, through prayer, or through some special ministry of the Spirit, believers experience God's presence in the midst of their suffering. Through the presence of the Spirit of glory, believers can even rejoice in their sufferings because they understand that God's purposes are being fulfilled.

"This name does not merely teach that the Holy Spirit is infinitely glorious Himself, but it rather teaches that He imparts the glory of God to us. . . . The Holy Spirit is the administrator of glory as well as of grace; or rather, He is the administrator of grace that culminates in glory." – R. A. Torrey.

interactive

Peter said believers are "insulted because of the name of Christ." These insults take many different forms. In the space provided, identify ways you have been insulted for your faith. How did the Spirit of glory give you strength and peace as you endured these insults? Were you able to bring glory to God through your responses?

Verbal Abuse _____

Reviled or Hated _____

Ridiculed _____

Slandered _____

discuss

What forms does religious persecution take today? When your faith causes others to ridicule or persecute you, how do you respond? Have you learned how to rejoice in the midst of suffering for your faith? How did the Spirit of glory strengthen you during times of persecution?

EXPECT PERSECUTION

Read John 15:18-21. Before His arrest, Jesus warned the disciples that the world would hate them because the world first hated Jesus. He explained that they should expect to be persecuted for their faith in Him because the world does not know God. As you journal below, consider: Are you surprised when people ridicule or reject you because of your faith in Christ? How does persecution emphasize your faithfulness to Christ? If you've never suffered for your faith, is it because you keep your faith hidden?

PAUSE to PRAY

Pray that your faith in Christ will be evident to others, even if it results in suffering. Ask God to strengthen your faith during these times so you might bring glory to Him.

All For God's Glory

When people profess their faith in Christ and receive the gift of salvation, they also receive the Holy Spirit. By walking in the Spirit at all times, believers become powerful witnesses for Christ. When controlled by the Spirit, everything they say and do brings glory to God. For obvious reasons, the world that hates Christ will persecute His faithful witnesses; therefore, Christians should not be surprised when they suffer various trials for their faith. In the midst of these distressing circumstances, Christians can rejoice because they are sharing the suffering of Christ. Through the presence of the

Spirit of glory, believers glimpse enough of God's glory to strengthen their faith and endure the persecution with the peaceful assurance that they will experience the full glory of God in heaven.

Jesus promised that the Holy Spirit would be given to His followers once Jesus has ascended to heaven to take His place at the right hand of God. Believers are sealed with the Spirit, marking them as God's possession, and symbolizing His promise of their inheritance—salvation and eternal life. Through the presence and power of the Spirit, all believers are equipped to establish His church, lead people to faith in Him, reach spiritual maturity, and bring glory to God. By relying upon the Spirit, believers have the ability to conquer their sinful natures and live holy lives that please God. By listening to the Spirit, believers are able to understand spiritual truths and wisely apply those truths to the specific situations in their lives. By depending on the Spirit, believers can shower God's agape love onto all people, even their enemies and tormentors, By allowing the Spirit to strengthen them during times of persecution, believers see God's glory for themselves and reveal His glory to others. The Holy Spirit is certainly Jesus' gift to His followers, for through the power of the Holy Spirit, believers bring praise, honor, and glory to God.

review

Believers receive strength for their ministry, especially during times of suffering and persecution, from the Spirit of glory. In return, as believers serve others in love and serve Christ though His church, they reveal God's glory to the world. Describe ways that the Spirit of glory has revealed Himself to you. How has the Spirit of glory encouraged you to persevere in your Christian walk when others ridicule or hate you? How can the Spirit of glory enable you to love those who hurt you or forgive those who offend you? What gifts have you received from the Spirit to enable you to fulfill the ministry calling that God has placed on your life? How does using those gifts for His service reveal God's glory to others?

SEEING GOD'S GLORY

Read Acts 7:54-60. Stephen boldly preached the gospel to an audience that violently rejected his message. In their fury, they dragged Stephen out of town and stoned him to death. In the final moments of his life, Stephen, filled with the Spirit, looked into heaven and saw the glory of God. As you journal below, consider: Do you allow fear to prevent you from sharing your faith? Have you suffered any type of persecution for your faith? How did the Spirit of glory strengthen your faith during that time?

PAUSE to PRAY

Thank God for allowing His Son to suffer for you. Pray that you will be willing to suffer hardship, ridicule, or persecution for your faith when necessary.

48